TRUMP

from

Published by Firefly Books Ltd. 2017

First printing

Publisher Cataloging-in-Publication Data (U.S.)

Library of Congress Control Number: 2017953734

Library and Archives Canada Cataloguing in Publication

Bourhis, Hervé, 1974-
[Trump de A à Z. English]
Trump : from A to Z / a primer by Hervé Bourhis ; translated from the French by Jacqueline Dinsmore ; with illustrations by: Rudy Spiessert [and 32 others].
Translation of: Trump de A à Z.
ISBN 978-0-228-10033-1 (softcover)
1. Trump, Donald, 1946- –Caricatures and cartoons. 2. Trump, Donald, 1946- –Humor. 3. Presidents–United States–Caricatures and cartoons. 4. Presidents–United States–Humor. I. Dinsmore, Jacqueline, 1951-, translator II. Spiessert, Rudy, 1974-, illustrator III. Title. IV. Title: Trump de A à Z. English
PN6231.T735B6813 2017 973.93302'07 C2017-905836-3

Published in the United States by
Firefly Books (U.S.) Inc.
P.O. Box 1338, Ellicott Station
Buffalo, New York 14205

Published in Canada by
Firefly Books Ltd.
50 Staples Avenue, Unit 1
Richmond Hill, Ontario L4B 0A7

Translator: Jacqueline Dinsmore

Printed in Canada

THE AUTHOR WOULD LIKE TO THANK MARTIN, NÉJIB, AND THE 17 FEMALE AND 17 MALE ILLUSTRATORS WHO CONTRIBUTED TO THE BOOK.

TRUMP from A to Z

a primer by

HERVÉ BOURHIS

Translated from the French by Jacqueline Dinsmore

With illustrations by:

RUDY SPIESSERT ★ RACHEL DEVILLE ★ ALEXIS BACCI-LEVEILLÉ ★ HERVÉ TANQUERELLE ★ MINI LUDVIN ★ ALEXANDRE CLÉRISSE ★ ZOÉ THOURON ★ AMÉLIE GRAUX ★ NATACHA SICAUD ★ TANGUI JOSSIC ★ THIBAUT SOULCIÉ ★ KARINE BERNADOU ★ ANOUK RICARD ★ HUGUES MICOL ★ DOROTHÉE DE MONFREID ★ TERREUR GRAPHIQUE ★ FRANÇOIS RAVARD ★ BRÜNO ★ FLORENCE DUPRÉ LA TOUR ★ LOÏC SÉCHERESSE ★ ANNE SIMON ★ MARION BILLET ★ CHRISTOPHE GAULTIER ★ CAPUCINE ★ CLÉMENTINE MÉLOIS ★ MARINE BLANDIN ★ ANTOINE MARCHALOT ★ PHILIPPE GIRARD ★ FRANÇOIS AYROLES ★ LISA MANDEL ★ WITKO ★ GRÉGORY MARDON ★ MARION MONTAIGNE

FIREFLY BOOKS

ABORTION

Trump has never been against abortion. He has always been liberal when it comes to morals. But his new ultra-conservative friends and his voters are pushing him to ban abortion, and he does not want to hurt their feelings.

• See: **Donald and Women**

ADDICTIONS

His brother Fred died of alcoholism, so Trump does not drink. He does not smoke either. He is only addicted to himself.

Surrealist expression invented by presidential counselor Kellyanne Conway in January 2017 to describe the lies of White House spokesperson Sean Spicer about the “record” crowd that attended Trump’s inauguration.
During the 2016 campaign, Trump had (among other “alternative” statements) belched out that Obama was Muslim, not American, ultimately backtracking, then denying having said anything like that. It doesn’t matter; the “info” was passed on to voters. That’s what’s important.

• See: **Plot, Hyperbole (Truthful), Inauguration, Trump Method**

For "alternative right," term created by Richard B. Spencer in 2008. A diverse group of neo-conservatives, Tea Party members, white supremacists, conspiracy theorists and other trolls of the American far right. They all prayed and worked for Trump's election.

· See: **Bannon, Conspiracy, KKK, Angry White Men, Trolls for Trump**

The slogan used by Trump during his campaign and his investiture ceremony symbolizing the protectionist program he has planned for the country. Hilarious parallel: "America First" was the name of a nationalist pro-Nazi party in the USA in 1943! LOL!

· See: **Keep America Great Again, Make America Great Again**

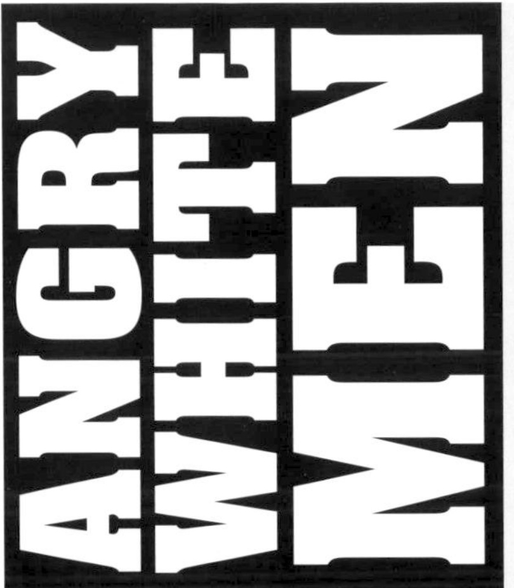

This election was undoubtedly one of the last in which this segment of the population, especially in the center of the country, will be heard. By 2050, minorities will have as much say as WASPs. It's called demographic change.
But then, Angry White Males are mostly the guys who have moved into the White House.
The message is clear: return to a patriarchy. Back to the pre-60s world.

·See: **Analyze, Trump Galaxy, Racism**

ANALYSIS

He became president thanks to his unique analysis of the American electoral map and the sociology of the country, when all the experts had him pegged a loser by a mile.

· See: **Endurance**

ATTENTION SPAN

3 minutes, according to those who know him.

Trump is THE anti-system candidate par excellence. The system is Washington. Well, Washington when he was not in power. The system is also money, but that was before he appointed people from Goldman Sachs around him. The system is Hollywood, with all those lefties. Well, except for Dory, a good American Hollywood fish. In short, the system is everything he dislikes or does not understand, because the world has revolved around him since 1946.

· See: **Galaxy Trump, Show Business**

BANKRUPTCY

"Stop saying I went bankrupt. I never went bankrupt but like many great business people have used the laws to corporate advantage—smart!"

— Donald Trump

He's filed at least six bankruptcies. In the 1990s, he almost didn't recover. The banks saved him. But then for a few years he was. . . A LOSER.
Otherwise, Trump has $950 million in mortgages with the Bank of China and Goldman Sachs.

See: **Business, Team, China**

BANNON
(STEPHEN OR STEVE)

The President's guru and strategic adviser is the only man allowed to enter the Oval Office without a tie, *"because it's Steve"*. . . Apart from these clothing considerations, the man has many talents. Ex-military, ex-banker at Goldman-Sachs (like everyone else at the White House. . .), this Islamophobic supremacist is the very influential chief of the website *Breitbart News*, the voice of the new American extreme right. When he was appointed to the National Security Council, he became the second most important figure in the U.S. It's like Darth Vader steering the Death Star, but worse.

The donkey cart had just entered the only street in Redneck Gulch. The fat, red-faced, blond man driving it suddenly began shouting, drawing a crowd: *"Buy into the Trump Solution! It will find you a job, give you dignity, build walls and grow hair!"* The inhabitants of this one-horse town knew he was a charlatan. But he was **their** charlatan.

The famous robe he wears to wander around the White House in the evening has its own Twitter account: @POTUSBathrobe

See: **White House**

BERLUSCONI

Trump and Italian media tycoon Berlusconi are exactly alike: they know how to appreciate themselves. Rich businessmen obsessed with bling and their virility, who came to power through television. Clearly liars. Heavy foundation make-up users. Berlusconi shattered democratic culture and Italian society, and clung to power like white on rice. Trump will not let his friend be king of the hill.

Rachel

GOLDEN GLUB
FAKE NEWS

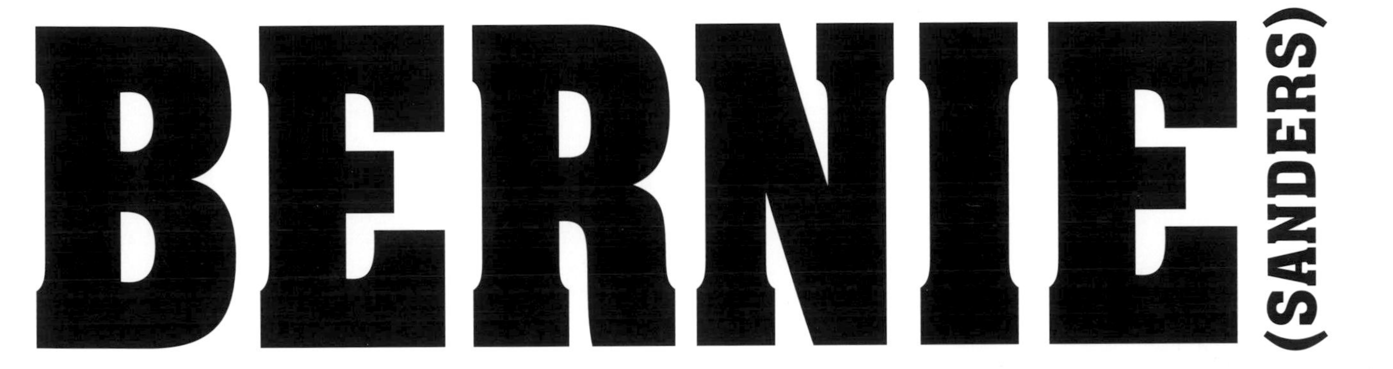

"We're a democracy, not a one-man show. We are not another Trump enterprise. It's called the United States of America."

—Bernie Sanders, Vermont senator

Would the anti-Trump camp, advocating American-style socialism, been elected if it had been backed instead of Hillary Clinton? We have eight years to think about it . . .

BIKERS FOR TRUMP

A fan club. On the other hand, there is no "Psychoanalysts for Trump." We checked.

· See: **Malicious Narcissism**

B

In the 19th century, Friedrich Trump—his German-American grandfather—owned saloons and brothels in Yukon and Alaska.

See: **Drumpf**

Ummm.... I don't think we are wanted here...

B

BUSINESS

Starting as a real estate agent with varying success, Donald truly became Trump when he started selling his image and his name for an incredible number of licenses. When Americans decided to buy every part of him to run their country, he had to hand his Trump Organization over to his children. He will manage "Company USA" in his own way, unless his fellow citizens finally say, "YOU'RE FIRED!"

TELEVISION

The Apprentice alone would have earned him some $200 million. As of September 2017, his total worth is $3.5 billion, according to Forbes.

REAL ESTATE

The symbol of this pastime (which he gradually abandoned after many reversals of fortune in the '90s) is the famous Trump Tower, showcase and base of his activities. The President often receives dignitaries at his own winter residence, the luxury complex Mar-a-Lago, in Palm Beach.

TRUMP ENTERTAINMENT RESORTS

This company was founded in 1995 and oversees the hotel and casino sectors of the organization. It has gone through 11 bankruptcies since 1985, including the famous casino hotel Trump Taj Mahal in Atlantic City, which eventually closed in 2016.

HE'S EVERYWHERE

Trump used to own the Miss USA and Miss Universe contests. He has invested in wrestling, American football. . . and there is also Trump Books, Trump University, Trump Winery, Trump Financial. . .

TRUMP LICENSING

Trump has sold his name for use on thousands of items. Vodka, whiskey, perfume (Success by Trump). There are also "Trump Steaks." Well-done, of course.

CALEXIT

In the traditionally progressive state of California, some have been considering secession since Trump was elected. The independent state would become the 6th world power! We can even imagine creating a new country with Oregon, the State of Washington and. . . Canada! The project will never come to pass, but it is symptomatic of the fragmentation that the country is experiencing. If this persists, Trump himself will end up creating a new State, "Trumpland," within Trump Tower!

CHINA

China, which is the frontrunner in globalization, is one of Trump's obsessions. "The concept of global warming was created by and for the Chinese," (he says) and the new administration has them in its sights. You would think he'd like a country that built a 6,000-mile wall. . .

Actually, he does. He's in the books for a $950 million loan from foreign lenders that include the state-owned Bank of China and Germany's Deutsche Bank.

• See: **Diplomacy, Great Wall of China**

C

CLIMATE CHANGE SKEPTICS

The Trump administration has no use for this green hipster nonsense that makes U.S. industry less competitive.

The President appointed Scott Pruitt, climate-skeptic activist, to head the Environmental Protection Agency.

· See: **Sioux**

CLINTON (HILLARY)

When Trump's unfortunate opponent came down on him heavily during the dirtiest campaign of all time, the billionaire suggested that she be put in prison and stated he wouldn't be sad if she caught a bullet. Then he returned the next day to say it was a joke. What a joker. LOL-NALD TRUMP!

Their mutual hatred is ferocious. But it hasn't always been like that.

The Clintons attended Donald and Melania's marriage in 2005. Hilarious pictures of the two couples are proof.

Trump, who called himself a Democrat at the time, was even a big donor to Hillary's senatorial campaign in 2000. . .

Sometimes The New York elite supports one another, sometimes they fight. They're only human.

· See: **Donald and Women**

$
Clérisse

CONSPIRACY THEORIES

Trump loves them. Obama was born in Kenya. ISIS was created by Hillary Clinton. Vaccines cause autism. Ted Cruz's father was involved in JFK's assassination. The White House has been infiltrated by incompetent fascists. . . Oops! No, that one's true.

CONFLICT OF INTEREST

· See: **Impeachment, Ivanka**

CONNECTED

Do you know many 70-year-olds who tweet so much, so impulsively? Who dominates television as well as social networks? Who also personifies and reflects our times?

· See: **Analysis, Television, Twitter**

CULT OF IGNORANCE

"... the false notion that democracy means that my ignorance is just as good as your knowledge."

—Isaac Asimov

Trump's America believes that too much education and contemplation harms the famous "common sense."

· See: **Idiocracy**

CULTURE, ARTS

(See page 3268)

zoéthouron

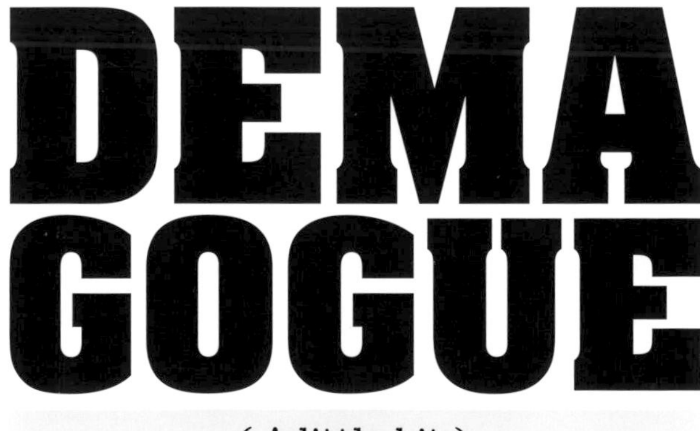

(A little bit.)

DEREGULATION

February 2017: Trump signs an executive order to remove the banking safeguards set up by Obama after the 2008 financial crisis. Trump owes this to the bankers who have bailed him out again and again following his successive bankruptcies. They look forward to the next crash with impatient excitement.

· See: **Bankruptcy**

DIPLOMACY

Putin is a nice guy. China is evil. Mexico is a parasite. Europe, NATO is finished. The Australians are losers. . . And, bang! 140 characters. (But everything can change. . . stay tuned.)

· See: **Europe, Snails**

DISRUPTION

Stephen Bannon's doctrine, approved by Trump. It's all about distancing themselves completely from previous administrations. Create chaos. Make a clean break. Build the Death Star.

· See: **Bannon**

DONALD (FIRST NAME)

Etymology: **He who reigns (Celtic).**
Origin: **Scottish.**
History: **Saint Donald of Ogilvy (8th century) transforms his house into a convent on the death of his wife, and his nine daughters become nuns. Then he invents the Miss Scotland contest and calls the parish priest a loser.**

DRUMPF

This is the real family name. They changed it to Trump after they arrived on American soil.

· See: **Bannon**

DONALD & WOMEN

“Nobody has more respect for women than me,” said Trump in 2016. Even though 43% of Americans who voted, voted for him, so it’s obviously a little more complicated than that . . .

· See: **Trump bashing**

HIS TEAM

Remember that incredible photo of Trump surrounded by a group of men as he signed the new anti-abortion decree? Trump may have appointed 14 men to key positions, but there are still many women in the White House. Betsy DeVos in Education (Wife of a military pal), Elaine Chao in Transport, and Linda McMahon in Small Business Administration. As well as the invaluable advisor and groupie, Kellyanne Conway, inventor of “alternative facts.”

WIVES

Donald Trump has been married three times. To Ivana, Marla and Melania. This last, a former top model, is the first First Lady to pose nude. But she is also the first to speak five languages.

MAMA TRUMP

Mary-Anne MacLeod Trump (1912-2000) fled Scottish misery for the New World. Once her husband Fred Trump became rich, she instilled in her willful son a taste for luxury and grandiloquence.

"... if Ivanka weren't my daughter, perhaps I'd be dating her."

DAUGHTERS

Trump is very proud of his daughters. Tiffany, the quiet one, had an excellent school career. But it was Ivanka (who, it is said, voted for Hillary Clinton) who was the cause of the first conflict of interest of his term, when the president tweeted, crying that a wicked chain of stores had stopped selling his little girl's products. Oh, and daddy's girl has taken the reins of the Trump Organization along with her brothers. . .

"Grab them by the pussy."

HILLARY

On January 20, 2017, President Trump asked for a standing ovation for Hillary Clinton, his ex-rival, who even attended the billionaire's inauguration. During the campaign, it was all: "If Hillary Clinton can't satisfy her husband, what makes her think she can satisfy America?" Not to mention, "Hillary wants to abolish, essentially abolish, the Second Amendment ... If she gets to pick her judges, nothing you can do, folks. Although the Second Amendment people, maybe there is, I don't know." But that was just a joke.

ENDURANCE

Still around after 30 years of conquering television, a few bankruptcies, an election campaign during which he endured the antagonism of the media, Democrats, his own party and the whole world, except Russia and Henry de Lesquen, France's vocal populist.

· See: **Trolls for Trump**

EARLY YEARS

Donald Trump was born in Queens, in the upscale neighborhood of Jamaica, one year after Bob Marley. The similarity ends there. His father, Fred Trump, made a fortune in real estate, and Donald grew up in a 23-room house with staff. At 13 years of age, the unruly lad was sent to a New York State military boarding school…

· See: **Heir**

EDUCATION

"Stopping Trump is a short-term solution. The long-term solution, which will be more difficult, is fixing the educational system that has created so many people ignorant enough to vote for Trump."

—Andy Borowitz
(writer, comedian)

EUROPE

Europe is finished, according to Trump.

Trump welcomed Brexit, criticized Germany for taking all those "illegals." France is completely decadent. And Brussels is "a beautiful city," but also a "hellhole." Trump knows Europe well; he built golf courses in Scotland. . .

· See: **Diplomacy, Snails**

FIRST LADY

Melania Trump, 47, is the president's third wife. A former model born in Slovenia, she is the first First Lady to have posed for erotic photos. Mrs. Nixon would never have done such a thing. Melania does not live in the White House, she has stayed in Manhattan with their son Barron.

· See: **Donald and women**

FAMILY

Donald is a fervent family man. He will not tolerate anyone attacking one of his four children. If you dare, the tweet machine will go to war.

· See: **Ivanka, Safari**

FORBES

In 2016, Donald Trump dropped 35 positions in Forbes' list of America's richest people and ended up 113th. His fortune is estimated at $3.5 billion, although he claims to have twice as much. Trump has appeared on the Forbes list since 1982. His name disappeared between 1990 and 1995, following successive real estate failures.

· See: **Business, Bankruptcy**

FOX NEWS

The voice of the American right wing.

· See: **Trump Galaxy**

We the People
tangui Jossic

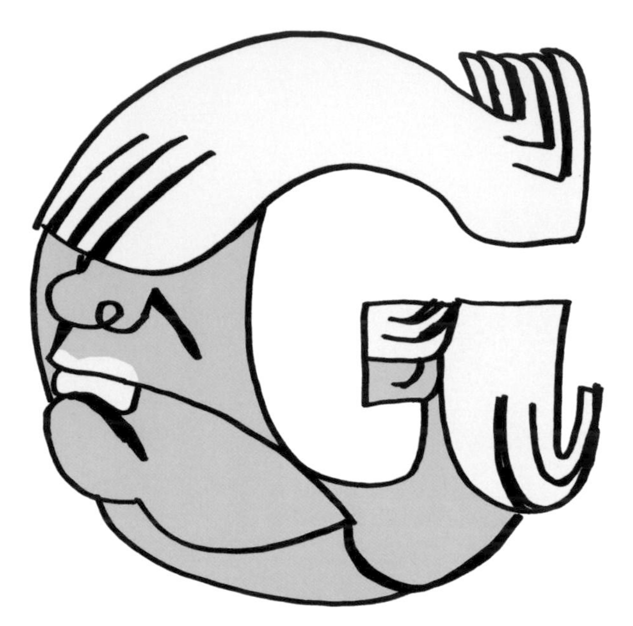

GENERAL LIABILITY

He was invited everywhere. He was America's favorite clown. The in-crowd thought him cool. But of course Trump was too much. So over the top. So off the wall.

· See: **Show business, Television**

GLOBALIZATION

Trump brand clothing is made in China. He invests in Dubai and Asia. He owns shares in Apple, whose smartphones he uses to tweet.

AND VOILA! HE'S CURED!
DR TRUMP
ELIXIR
FOR GLOBALI-ZATION
$$$
Soulcié

G

GODFATHER (THE)

His favorite film along with Citizen Kane. Now that's believable. Favorite quote: "It's not personal, Sonny. It's strictly business."

Trump was, in turn, a democrat, independent and republican, depending which way the wind blew. The Grand Old Party did not want Trump as a candidate. His popularity with the grassroots said otherwise. Will the GOP Big Cheeses have the courage to tackle him, now that he's in power?

GOLD STAR FAMILY

The day Trump almost lost the election. On August 1, 2016, Clinton maintained he criticized the Muslim family of an American hero who died in war. The country exploded. Changing times: he was able to survive the ordeal with no problems.

· See: **Vietnam**

GRIZZLIES

During Betsy DeVos's surreal hearing before the Senate to become Secretary of Education, she said she would like to allow weapons in schools in some states so that students can defend themselves against grizzly bears. One can't help but wonder who will defend the grizzlies against the Trump administration.

G

TRUMP GALAXY

They orbit around the Orange Star. Friends, models, disciples, groupies, collaborators, conspiracy trolls... savoring this moment when America finally becomes their America.

MEDIA

Fox News is the official organ of Trumpism. As well as Steve Bannon's Breitbart News website and the radical right 2.0 conglomerate.

ADVISORS

Steve "You're fired, too!" Bannon was his ideologist, so now he listens to Alex Jones, the chief conspiracy theorist. For the economy, former Goldman-Sachsian Anthony Scaramucci has his ear. And for communication and strategy, the wonderful Kellyanne Conway is still there, at least until she makes one blunder too many.

MODELS

Young Donald's mentor was Roy Cohn, friend of the Mafia. Trump also admires Joseph McCarthy, the anti-communist, and strongmen like Putin, Reagan and Churchill. Arnold Schwarzenegger, too, at one time, but they're now on the outs.

SUPPORT

Besides the paleoconservatives and the wrestling federation, the KKK supported Trump during the campaign, as well as the NRA (Trump signed the end of the ban on the sale of weapons to the mentally ill. . .). And don't forget WikiLeaks and Julian Assange. . .

PEOPLE

Clint Eastwood, Chuck Norris (obviously), Moe Tucker (from the Velvet Underground), Kanye West, Nicole Kidman and Matthew McConaughey (Trump spies?). . .

FANS

The Trumpettes is a fan club created by Toni Holt Kramer, a former TV star and Trumpette extraordinaire. "He's a Superman-hero hovering around, waiting to come down at the right moment – now my Superman-hero has landed."

His secret? Helmet Head Extra Firm Hairspray ($ 11.99).
And a few implants.

HANDSHAKE

As this book goes to print, only Justin Trudeau (who's not a bad boxer) was able to withstand Trump's "gorilla handshake."

· See: **Putin**

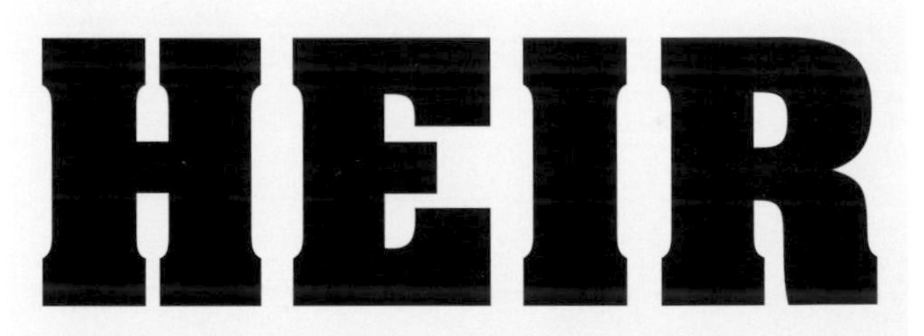

In 1971, at 25, he took over the family business and became a millionaire.

· See: **Childhood, Self-Made Man**

HOUSE OF CARDS (SERIES)

Can't touch the real thing. No writer could have imagined what is going on in the White House right now. And Francis Underwood is down for the count.

Expression created by Tony Schwartz, Trump's ghostwriter, in *The Art of the Deal*, the billionaire's bestseller. "It's an innocent form of exaggeration — and a very effective form of promotion." Not unlike the famous "Reality Distortion Field" cherished by Steve Jobs, another great perverse narcissistic manipulator, but in a more hippie way.

See: **Alternative Facts, Conspiracy, Evil Narcissism, The Art of the Deal.**

H

IDIOCRACY

In Mike Judge's 2006 far-seeing satire, we discover the U.S. of the future, eroded by anti-intellectualism, mercantilism, junk food and the destruction of the environment. The president is an arrogant former wrestler who screams all the time.

• See: **Cult of Ignorance, Zoolander**

IMMIGRATION

Trump wants to expel 11 million undocumented immigrants. Even if he has used thousands on his construction sites for decades... It is estimated that these expulsions would cost $400 billion. It would take 84 buses and 47 planes every day for two years. Not counting the famous wall.

• See: **Wall**

IMPEACHMENT

The famous threat of removal, which made Nixon resign! The dream of Trump's opponents. But it's an extremely complex process. What would his Watergate be? Or, rather, his Yellow-Watergate? He may have turned his business operations over to his children, but his many potential conflicts of interest will eventually bring about his impeachment. But we can't see him resigning, like that loser Nixon. Trump never admits defeat...

• See: **Urinegate**

NRA
Anouk Ricard

"A Gothic nightmare." We're a long way from the 2008 bash with Aretha Franklin. Despite official denials, there was, according to police calculations, a smaller crowd than for Obama (when roughly 1.5 million people showed), but still quite a few (around 400,000). Trump struggled to bring in celebrities. In the end, it was the star of a reality TV show, Jackie Evancho, who sang the national anthem.

· See: **Alternative facts, Trump bashing**

ISRAEL

Since 1947, POTUS has been a friend of Israel. "I am 100% with Israel." Trump certainly has a super strategy to solve the Israeli-Palestinian conflict, even though at the time this book was published, it seemed confusing. Oh wait, he doesn't actually have one.

· See: **Religion, POTUS**

IVANKA

February 2017: when a chain of luxury stores stopped selling his daughter Ivanka's shoes, Trump published a distressed tweet. Problem: he is the president of the United States and it is a conflict of interest. Ivanka and her brothers, Donald Jr. and Eric, inherited Dad's business when he became POTUS. Politically, Daddy's little girl is closer to Hillary Clinton! How ungrateful can you get! And he funded the best detox treatments for her.

· See: **Donald and women**

"I will be the greatest jobs president that God ever created."

If only it were true.

JOURNALISM

Very dishonest, according to Trump and his friends.
In any case, Trump and his people no longer believe in the future of traditional mass media. From now on, info will be transmitted through social networks, targeting the message very precisely based on the audience. No need for a hostile intermediary.

"The media should be embarrassed and humiliated and keep its mouth shut and just listen for a while."

— Steve Bannon, January 2017

JUSTICE

Trump and his companies have been involved in 3,500 court cases. This is due to his obvious disregard for laws, notably labor laws, but also because he is litigious to the extreme. He loves the sport so much that if he could sue himself, he would.

· See: **Trump University**

Trump bestowing full employment (Allegory)

Trump has already filed this slogan away for re-election in 2020.

· See: **America First, Make America Great Again**

KITSCH

Like his buddies the Russian nouveau riche, Trump loves everything vulgar, massive, gilded and flashy. His 32,291 ft² 3-story is so Rococo that just looking at photos can blind you. Sobriety, asceticism and minimalism is fine for losers like Steve Jobs or those pathetic Tibetan monks.

· See: **Trump Force One**

KKK

In August 2016, the Ku Klux Klan, through its leader David Duke, announced its support for the Donald Trump campaign. Trump may say he's not familiar with this group (though we know his father participated in at least one of their demonstrations. . .) but his son Eric has stated, "The guy does deserve a bullet. . . These are horrible people." Or maybe lynch them?

· See: **Alt-right**

Something to be circumvented. Good for others.

In 2011, 44% of Americans without higher education answered YES to a research institute's question: *"Would you support a strong leader who would not have to deal with Congress or be subject to elections?"*

· See: **Quotes, Tyrant?**

LITERATURE

A number of books have become bestsellers since his election. *1984* (1949) by Orwell of course, *The Man in the High Castle* (1962) by Philip K. Dick, about a Japanese-Nazi dictatorship in the USA... And don't forget *It Can't Happen Here* (1935), where Sinclair Lewis describes a fascist dictatorship in the USA, or Robert Penn Warren's *Les Fous du roi* (1946), that recounts the advent of an American populist leader.

· See: **Tyrant?**

LGBT

In the past, Trump made donations for the fight against AIDS and opened real estate programs for gay couples. After the Orlando massacre, he supported the gay community (in order to escalate tirades against the Muslim community). But then he chose homophobic Mike Pence as vice-president...

This slogan was stolen from Reagan, who used it in 1980. But Trump registered it in 2012. . . as a slogan and trademark for caps, ties, t-shirts, etc.

· See: **Keep America Great Again, Reagan**

make Amerikkka great again!
"DON'T WORRY, THE FUTURE IZ BEHIND US"
HOME
HOME
HOME
TEXACO PRESENTE
PREZ
TEXAS
terreur

MANAGEMENT

So the idea is to run a country like you run a business. With Disneyland as the Center of Excellence?

• See: **Bankruptcy**

MARCHES

From the first days of his term of office, after his orders on abortion, and restricting entry to the country for nationals of certain Muslim countries, massive demonstrations sprung up all over the country. Less so in Alabama.

Roy Cohn was a lawyer for the Mafia, Joseph McCarthy at the height of McCarthyism and the Trump family. But Trump cut all ties with the man who had been his mentor and advisor since childhood, when the lawyer confessed to having AIDS (He died in 1986).

· See: **Trump Galaxy**

METHOD

Get criticized. Launch an unduly excessive counter-attack, with lots of screaming. Then, once the hysteria has passed, concede and negotiate out of sight of the cameras.

· See: **Racism**

According to Trump, Mexicans are dealers and rapists. They are "bad hombres." They will pay for the wall that Trump wants to build along the border.

· See: **Trump University, Wall**

MUSLIM BAN

M

On February 1, 2017, Trump triggered an outcry by signing an antiterrorist order refusing access to the U.S. for nationals of Iraq, Iran, Libya, Somalia, Sudan, Syria and Yemen.

But not for Dubai, Turkey, Egypt, Saudi Arabia or the United Arab Emirates. Even though these countries are often linked to terrorism. Ah, but they do business with the Trump Organization.

After the Muslim ban and the court ruling against him, Trump tweeted about justice from the politicized "so-called judge."

· See: **Justice, Protests**

NEW YORKER (THE)

The weekly is without doubt Trump's No. 1 opponent. Goddamn Obamist New York intellectual bastards!

· See : **Trump bashing**

NARCISSISM (MALICIOUS)

This is what psychiatrists call the syndrome afflicting Donald Trump.And Dr. John D. Gartner has launched a petition for the removal of the president, convinced that Trump is mentally incapable of performing his functions.

· See : **Bikers for Trump**

N

1984

NINETEEN EIGHTY FOUR

Big Orange Brother is watching you?

· See: **Literature**

Quiz: Does the National Rifle Association support President Trump?

A. **Definitely.**

B. **Enthusiastically.**

C. **Bang! Bang!**

NUCLEAR (FORCE)

"I genuinely believe that if Trump wins and gets the nuclear codes, there is an excellent possibility it will lead to the end of civilization."
—Tony Schwartz (ghostwriter)

· See: **The Art of the Deal**

N

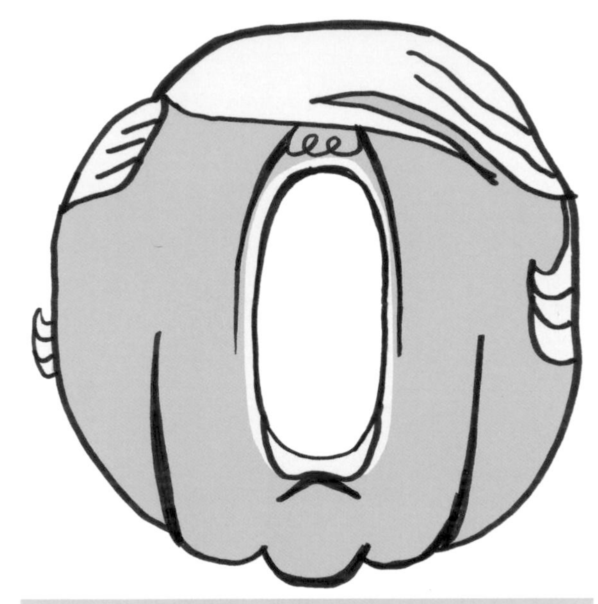

OBAMA (BARACK)

"Obama will go down as the worst President in history on many topics but especially foreign policy."

(Trump Tweet from September 12, 2012)

OBAMACARE

He promised. On his arrival in the White House, Trump signed an executive order to unravel Obamacare, the symbol of the Obama presidency that the alt-right compared to the final solution. . . Trump promised to make a better health system for less. Once in the White House, however, he warned that it might take longer and be more complicated than expected. No kidding!

OLD

At 70 years old, Donald Trump is the oldest president ever elected to the White House.

ORANGE

"*Orange is the new black.*"
(Mythical tweet by Amol Rajan the day the Obama successor was elected.)

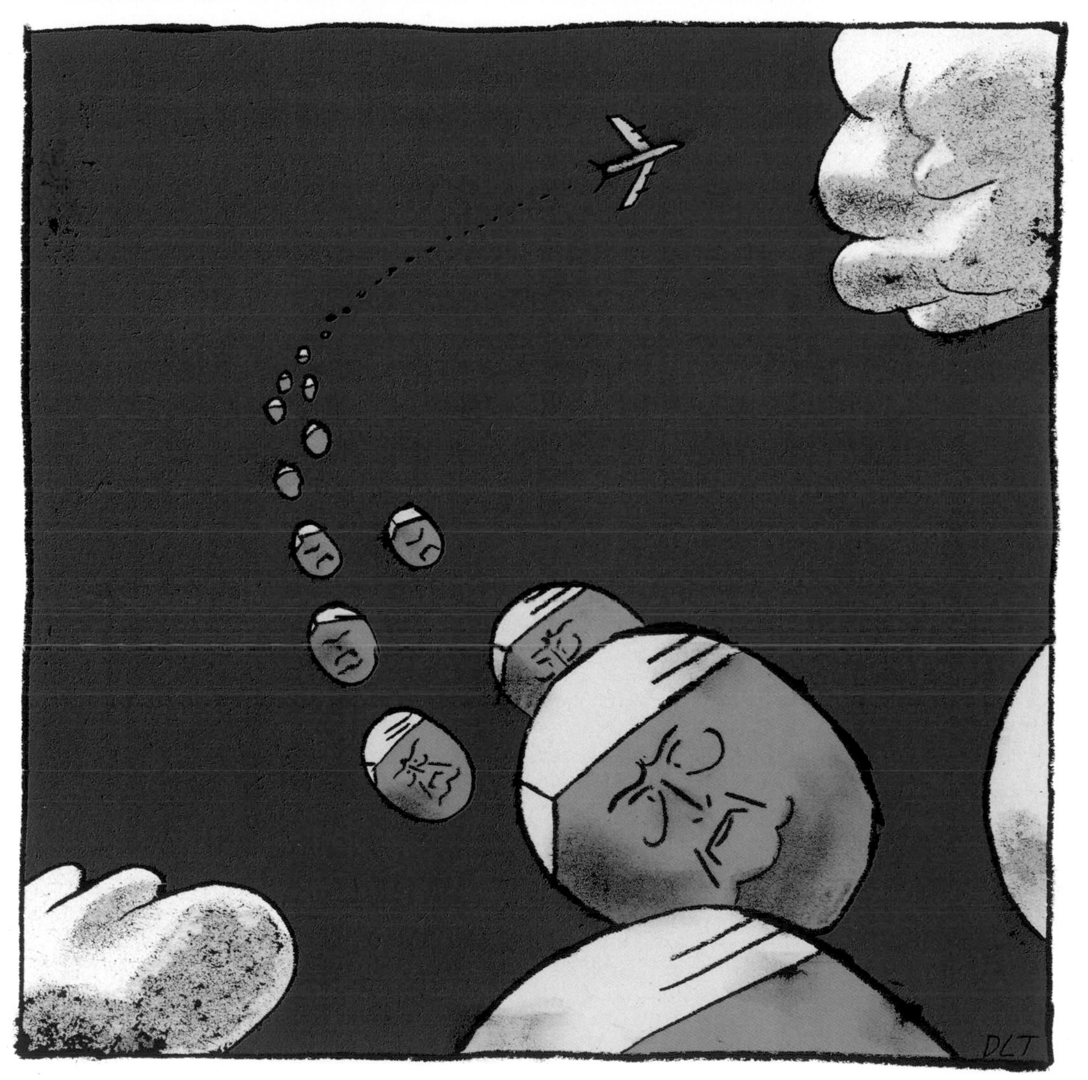

2017: Worldwide spread of Agent Orange

PLEBISCITE?

The "people's candidate" received nearly 3 million fewer votes than Hillary Clinton. Trump is the president of the Electoral College and small states.

· See: **Analysis**

PIG (PUTTING LIPSTICK ON ONE)

How Tony Schwartz describes his ghostwriting work for Trump.

· See: **The Art of the Deal**

POOR (THE)

Truly poor Americans do not vote for Trump or Clinton. Not even for Bernie Sanders. They don't vote.

· See: **Clinton, Angry White Men, Sanders**

P

A smidgeon.

POST-TRUTH

· See: **Alternative facts, Hyperbole (Truthful)**

In the 1990 video *Sleep Now in the Fire* by the funk-metal band Rage Against the Machine, a guy is seen carrying a "DONALD J. TRUMP FOR PRESIDENT 2000" sign.

· See: **Pop icon**

POTUS

The acronym for "President of the United States."

PUSSY (GRAB)

Seduction tutorial by Donald Trump (2005): "Grab 'em by the pussy." The revelation of this horrible phrase created such an outcry that Trump was not elected. Oh wait, yes he was.

· See: **Donald and Women**

DON'T EVEN THINK ABOUT IT
Anne Simon

Meow!

P

Trump admires and systematically defends Putin, the strong man, "the one who rides bears." Even when Russia is suspected of cyber-attacking the United States. Oddly enough, it is very similar to the name of the national dish from Justin Trudeau's country, the other neighbor that Trump doesn't admire and criticizes regularly.

· See: **Grizzlies, Handshake**

POP ICON

Beginning in the 1980s, Donald Trump built a reputation as the cartoonish mascot of capitalism's worst characteristics: materialism, greed, and cutthroat finance, crowned with his "You're Fired!" mantra. Now (astonishingly) the President of the United States, Trump's triumphs have become more abundant, more ambitious, and more political. Here is a collection of Trumpisms up to 2016.

TELEVISION

In 35 years, Trump has been prominent on American television, from *Saturday Night Live* to shopping channels. Perhaps most memorable, Jimmy Fallon rumpling Trump's notorious hair in 2015 and Donald Trump bodyslamming fighter Vince McMahon at Wrestlemania XXIII in 2007. As for TV series, Trump appeared on *The Simpsons*, *The Fresh Prince of Bel-Air*, *The Nanny*... And of course, he was the producer and host of *The Apprentice* for 14 years!

PUBLICITY

In the 90s we saw him in ads for McDonald's, Oreo, Pizza Hut, Visa...

BOOKS

Dozens of novels mention Trump, the most famous being *American Psycho* by Bret Easton Ellis (1991) in which the story's serial killer protagonist is obsessed with the billionaire, who is mentioned 25 times!

CINEMA

Trump has been appearing since 1992 in cameo roles (*Home Alone 2*). He has appeared in a dozen films, including *Zoolander*, *Wall Street 2*, *54* and *Celebrity* (by Woody Allen). And he inspired the character of Biff Tannen in *Back to the Future 2*.

BOARD GAMES

Trump: the Game, inspired by Monopoly, was released in 1989.
The goal of the game was to. . . uhm. . . earn money.

SONGS

Trump has been quoted thousands of times in American songs, notably in rap. "Donald Trump" by Mac Miller (2011), "Donald Trump's Hair" by Kacey Jones (2009) and "Donald Trump" (Black Version) by The Time and a song written by. . . Prince!

QUOTES
(QUOTATIONS, ANTHOLOGY)

"It's freezing and snowing in New York—we need global warming!"

"The point is that you can't be too greedy."

"Forget love. It's time to get tough."

"I thought being President would be easier than my old life."

Q

RACISM

The first time the country heard of Donald Trump was in 1973: The NY TIMES announced that a leading 26-year-old real estate developer was accused of discriminating against people of color in one of his housing projects. His defense was ready. . . He replied by condemning anti-white racism and sued for $100 million (He finally folded and signed a court consent decree). But since this story, Trump has not appeared particularly racist, as long as you don't count that whole Charlottesville thing. . .

"Sad that there are more black people in Beyoncé right now, than in Trumps [sic] entire cabinet team." (Tweet by comedian Gráinne Maguire when Beyoncé announced she was pregnant with twins)

· See: **Team, Angry White Men**

RAP

Trump and rap go back a long way! Hated by Eminem and Tupac, he is admired by other rappers for his misogyny and his success. Kanye West wanted to meet him at Trump Tower the day after his election for a nice little selfie. Genius.com has listed 6,069 references to Trump in rap songs. And that was before his election...

· See: **Pop icon**

REAGAN (RONALD)

The leader of the 1980–88 conservative revolution had much in common with Trump. Famous from the silver screen. Angry with the truth. Despised by his party (Republican, too). Nationalist. Vain. Warmonger. Then again, he had experience in politics. And did not seem to have psychological problems.

· See: **Make American Great Again**

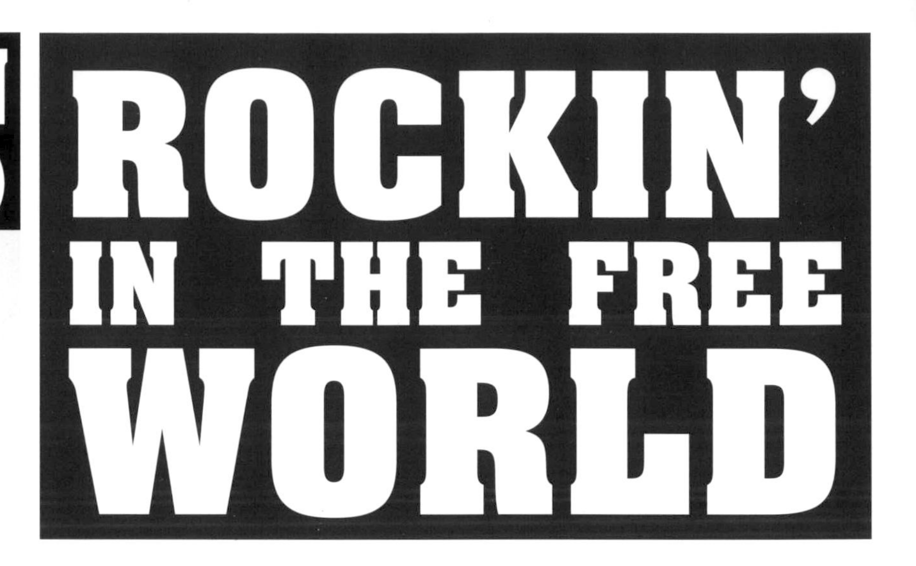

Neil Young, a supporter of Bernie Sanders, wasn't very happy that Trump used his song, without permission, during his campaign.

Mormons don't like Donald Trump's "false faith." During the campaign, Pope Francis reckoned Donald Trump was not a good Christian. Trump was shocked. Who does the Pope think he is? The Christianity-police? Actually, Trump is close to the Reformed Church of Preacher Norman Vincent Peale, author of the bestselling *The Power of Positive Thinking*. He supports and is supported by "Prosperity Gospel" televangelists, who believe that God rewards deserving people with material wealth. Bingo! Sounds great.

· See : **Isreal, Muslim ban**

SAFARI

When photos of the Trump sons killing leopards in Africa were posted online, Dad did not see what the problem was. So now we will have to apologize for bumping off protected species? Thank you, political correctness.

• See: **Family**

SCHWARZENEGGER (ARNOLD)

In between meetings, the new president trashed his replacement in *The Apprentice*, (the former governor of California), because the Terminator's ratings were lower. Schwarzy replied: "Hey Donald, I have a great idea—why don't we switch jobs? And then people can finally sleep comfortably again."

Did you ever imagine that one day you'd prefer Schwarzenegger as president instead of the current one. . .

• See: **The Apprentice**

Capucine

SELF MADE MAN

He’s not one.

· See: **Early Years**

SEXISM

· See: **Donald and Women**

SHOW BUSINESS

What is the difference between modern politics and reality TV? Nothing. Trump has understood this for a long time. Obama, too. And the Kennedys, who displayed their (false) family happiness, what was that?

· See: **General liability, Television**

SIOUX

The Lakota (a Sioux band) have gone on the warpath since Trump relaunched the construction of oil pipelines on their territory. . . In February 2017, they set fire to their protest camp after months of protest against the federal decision breaching all current treaties. Trump did not care. Most Native Americans voted for Sanders.

SNAILS

In 2015, Trump wanted to pave over a part of the Scottish coast to build a golf course bearing his name, of course. But Europe refused, as the rocks were home to a very rare species of snails. So Europeans are pathetic. And gastropods are losers.

• See: **Team**

STUPIFIED

That November morning when you learned that no, Hillary Clinton had not won.

Anecdote: They say that during their first week at the White House, Trump's advisors met in a dark Cabinet Room, as they hadn't yet found the light switch. It's near the door.

• See: **White House**

SUPER RICH (THE)

The president believes billionaires are the solution. Well, obviously! They're not the problem! How can people that represent only 1% of the population be a problem? It's basic math. Use your brain!

· See: **Team**

S

TAXES

This businessman did not pay any for 18 years, thanks to his lawyers who specialize in tax optimization. Even today we know nothing about the subject, as he is the only candidate for 45 years who has refused to reveal his tax returns.

TEAM (HIS)

It's made up of white billionaires, former military men or Goldman Sachs alumni. Or even all three.

· See: **Trump Galaxy**

People have had Trump's face tattooed on their skin.

Yes. People did that.

TELEVISION

During his campaign, Trump did not need to pay for a lot of TV ads to introduce himself to Americans. They had known him inside and out for 30 years, ever-present on television, hammering home his winner catchphrases. He was part of the furniture. Since the 80s, Trump has embodied the American Dream. Like Sinatra, Elvis, Marilyn, Dylan. . .

· See: **Endurance, Responsibility, The Apprentice**

THE APPRENTICE

25 million Americans watched the final episode of the reality TV show that starred Trump. A witch's brew of brutal bullying along with the requisite sadism and public humiliation. What's not to love?

· See: **Schwarzenegger, You're fired!**

THE ART OF THE DEAL

Trump has published several bestsellers (which he didn't write, of course). The first, The Art of the Deal (1987), spent 51 weeks at the top of the book charts in the U.S. when it came out. Tony Schwartz, his ghostwriter, is angry with himself for helping Trump develop his "ideas" and describes Trump as a "black hole" (among other things).

· See: **Hyperbole (Truthful), Management, Pig**

TOWER

Trump Tower in Manhattan is 58 stories high. In a, shall we say, luxuriant style. This is where the Trump family lives. And this is the seat of the Trump Organization. In order to protect the president and his family when they are there, the Pentagon leases one floor for $1.5 million a year (special family price). Oh, yes, and the 58th floor is called. . . the 68th. So people often think that the building is 68 stories high. Clever.

· See: **Family, Hyperbole (Truthful), White House**

In 1987, 1999 and 2011, he almost ran for office. But the country wasn't ready. Him? Yes. Trump is always ready.

· See: **Prophecy**

TROLLS FOR TRUMP

France's alt-right like Trump. "Pepe the Frog," a benign meme created by Matt Furie, has become, to his chagrin, the mascot for the extreme right 2.0 who rage in online forums. They say that Trolls for Trump influenced the 2016 campaign with their activism on social networks. Their official organization is Breitbart, Steve Bannon's fake news factory, which will soon have a French branch. Cool!

· See: **Alt-right, Bannon**

"STINKY FAT ASS." ONE S OR TWO?
THIS IS FOR A TWEET TO VALERY GISCARD D'ESTAING.
HE TRASHED MY NEW EARRING.
I DON'T KNOW MR. DONALD, IT'S PROBABLY A CONSPIRACY.
MARCHALOT

T

TWAIN (MARK)

"All you need in this life is ignorance and confidence, and then success is sure."

· See: **Forbes**

TWITTER

Trump, a tweet-addict, has posted 34,500 messages since 2009. On every subject. Foreign policy or Meryl Streep, "one of the most over-rated actresses in Hollywood." We hoped he would stop once he got to the White House. Nope. They say Trump is the first president to campaign primarily on social networks. Wrong—it was Obama in 2008.

· See: **Connected, White-House, Quotes**

TYRANT?

"He just could not help himself." Historian Tom Holland has compared Trump to the Roman emperor Caligula who breathed spectacle and conceit. He had an enormous six-horse chariot drive him around Rome. He trampled the elite with insults, mockery and humiliation. Outraged that the Roman senators had power, he ridiculed and belittled them. He despised traditional values. . . they got in the way. But Caligula had enemies. He told a captain in the guard that he sounded like a girl. And the guard killed him.

As for Nero. He was the despot who set fire to Rome. They said he was insane.

· See: **Narcissism (Malicious)**

PHILIPPE
GIRARD

TRUMP BASHING

Donald Trump was voted in by the Electoral College, but he holds the record in unpopularity for a newly installed president. Of course, he thinks this is just fine. Everything is good as long as they're talking about him. . .

· See: **Donald and women**

HOLLYWOOD

Meryl Streep, described by Trump as an "over-rated actress," took the lead in anti-Trump Hollywood baiting. Alec Baldwin found a second life as his official impersonator on *Saturday Night Live*.

TWEETS FROM THE DAY FOLLOWING TRUMP'S VICTORY

"Flash: In the event of a Donald Trump victory, France will demand the return of the Statue of Liberty." (@legorafi)

"Have you ever seen a whole country fail an IQ test?" (@KwesMat)

"I'm trying to form a government. Is there a tutorial or something on YouTube?" (@vraiDonaldTrump)

THE WOMEN

The massive demonstrations in January 2017 against the anti-abortion decrees were a first warning for the Trump administration. The mostly women protestors said they will stay in the street for four years if necessary. . . eight, according to Trump. The Prez went down to the street once. . . but it was to unveil his star on Hollywood Boulevard, which by the way had been damaged.

MICHAEL MOORE

One of Trump's most famous opponents, Michael Moore, had predicted his victory. Sadly, the baseball-hat prophet also predicted that the Electoral College would not vote for him, which proved inaccurate.

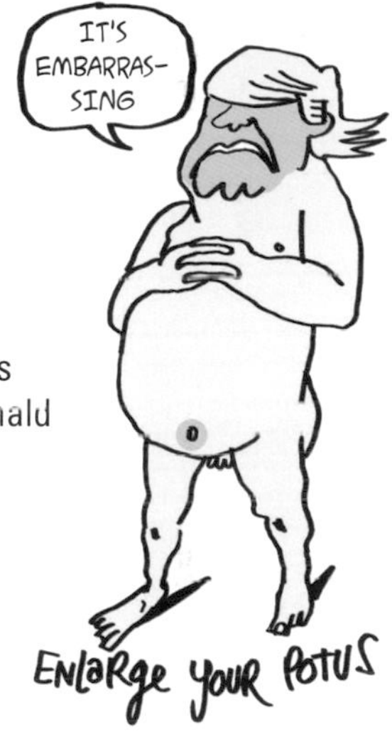

THE EMPEROR HAS NO BALLS

In August 2016, an anarchist collective illegally erected life-size statues in various American cities representing a naked Donald Trump with a micropenis. . . to match his microhands, one can only guess.

MEDIA

In an unprecedented move, the Trump White House banned some newspapers and magazines from press briefings! In retaliation, the *New York Times* launched a campaign against Trump's alternative facts. *The New Yorker* resolutely declared war. Its artistic director, Françoise Mouly, even started a free anti-Trump feminist publication called *Resist!*.

(TRUMP) UNIVERSITY

The "university," which taught students about real estate and entrepreneurship for a fortune, closed in 2010 following a lawsuit for fraud and bogus education. Always those blasted regulations! Note that Federal Judge Curiel, who heard the case, was of Mexican origin. . .

· See: **Endurance, Responsibility, The Apprentice**

UNPREDICTABLE

The billionaire president may have changed everything by the time you read these lines. Or he will have done the opposite of what he tweeted. Or tweeted the opposite of what he didn't say. While all the time denying it. It's the discreet charm of the Trumpery.

URINE GATE

The rumor of the existence of a Russian sex tape showing the president quite adept at urinophile games. Don't eat the yellow snow!

· See: **XXX**

I hear it's tough to get in.
What are we supposed to ignore again?
I worked all weekend to unlearn everything.
TRUMP
UNIVERSITY
FRANÇOIS AYROLES

U

VIETNAM

Thanks to a bone spur that made him unfit for service, Trump missed the Vietnam War. That didn't stop him from calling senator and war hero John McCain a loser because he was taken prisoner and tortured by the Vietcong in 1968.

· See: **Gold Star Family**

VOCABULARY

Very limited, essentially binary:
Winners/Losers
Excellent/Very bad
Big/Small
Stupid/Great.

Pro: **Easy to understand by everyone.**
Con: **Sometimes not quite enough to describe the complexity of facts.**

Pro: **Facts don't exist.**
Con: **Seeing problems everywhere = conspiracy theories.**

U

WALK OF FAME

Donald Trump has a star on the Hollywood sidewalk. It was vandalized in October 2016, and since restored.

• See: **General liability, Show Business**

WALL

Roger Waters (ex-Pink Floyd) wants to do his show The Wall at the USA and Mexico border. In protest.

• See: **Immigration, Mexico**

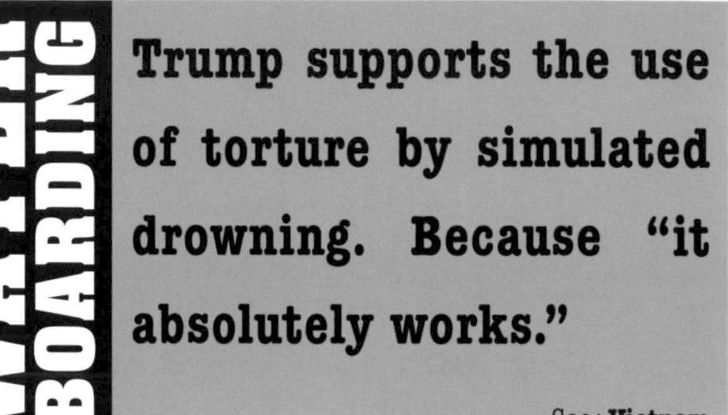

WATER BOARDING

Trump supports the use of torture by simulated drowning. Because "it absolutely works."

• See: **Vietnam**

WHITE HOUSE (ATMOSPHERE)

The White House neo-tenants' first weeks have been described as chaotic. Several teams that hated each other, winging it, leaks, betrayals. . . Trump, without his wife or children, would spend his evenings in a bathrobe, watching the news channels, tweeting and exploring the far corners of the building.

• See: **Team, Galaxy Trump, Surrealism, Twitter**

Lisa Mandel

X

During his campaign, Trump said he wanted to ban porn. But in 2000, he made an appearance in a Playboy movie and seems to have long been attracted by XXX actresses. . .

· See: **Pop icon**

Y

YOU'RE FIRED!

His iconic punch line in *The Apprentice*. A lot of Americans are waiting for the moment they can say it to him!

· See: **Schwarzenegger, The Apprentice**

ZOOLANDER

Trump appears in Ben Stiller's film. He plays himself, like David Bowie, a lesser-known star.

· See: **Idiocracy, Pop icon**

Z